# THE ETHIOPIAN FAMINE

by
**Elizabeth Glaser**

Illustrations by
**Brian McGovern**

**LUCENT**
B·O·O·K·S

**WORLD DISASTERS**

These and other titles are available in the Lucent World Disasters Series:

| | |
|---|---|
| The Armenian Earthquake | The Ethiopian Famine |
| The Bhopal Chemical Leak | The Hindenburg |
| The Black Death | Hiroshima |
| The Challenger | The Irish Potato Famine |
| Chernobyl | Krakatoa |
| The Chicago Fire | Pompeii |
| The Crash of 1929 | The San Francisco Earthquake |
| The Dust Bowl | The Titanic |

**Library of Congress Cataloging-in-Publication Data**

Glaser, Elizabeth
    The Ethiopian famine / by Elizabeth Glaser ; illustrations by
Brian McGovern.
        p. cm. — (World disasters)
    Includes bibliographical references (p.    ).
    Includes index.
    Summary: Discusses the Ethiopian famine of the 1980s within its
historical, geographical, and political contexts and examines the
possibility of future famines there.
    ISBN 1-56006-014-X
    1. Famines—Ethiopia—Juvenile literature. 2. Climatic changes—
Ethiopia—Juvenile literature. [1. Famines—Ethiopia.]
I. McGovern, Brian, ill. II. Title. III Series.
HC845.Z9F342   1990
363.8'0963—dc20                                                      90-6247
                                                                            CIP
                                                                            AC

*To my husband, Jeff Luther,*
*for his help in researching this book.*

# Table of Contents

# Preface
# The World Disasters Series

World disasters have always aroused human curiosity. Whenever news of tragedy spreads, we want to learn more about it. We wonder how and why the disaster happened, how people reacted, and whether we might have acted differently. To be sure, disaster evokes a wide range of responses—fear, sorrow, despair, generosity, even hope. Yet from every great disaster, one remarkable truth always seems to emerge: in spite of death, pain, and destruction, the human spirit triumphs.

History is full of disasters, arising from a variety of causes. Earthquakes, floods, volcanic eruptions, and other natural events often produce widespread destruction. Just as often, however, people accidentally bring suffering and distress on themselves and other human beings. And many disasters have sinister causes, like human greed, envy, or prejudice.

The disasters included in this series have been chosen not only for their dramatic qualities, but also for their educational value. The reader will learn about the causes and effects of the greatest disasters in history. Technical concepts and interesting anecdotes are explained and illustrated in inset boxes.

But disasters should not be viewed in isolation. To enrich the reader's understanding, these books present historical information about the time period, and interesting facts about the culture in which each disaster occurred. Finally, they teach valuable lessons about human nature. More acts of bravery, cowardice, intelligence, and foolishness are compressed into the few days of a disaster than most people experience in a lifetime.

Dramatic illustrations and evocative narrative lure the reader to distant cities and times gone by. Readers witness the awesome power of an exploding volcano, the magnitude of a violent earthquake, and the hopelessness of passengers on a mighty ship passing to its watery grave. By reliving the events, the reader will see how disaster affects the lives of real people and will gain a deeper understanding of their sorrow, their pain, their courage, and their hope.

## Introduction

# The Face of Hunger

A close-up of the face of an Ethiopian child fills the TV screen. Her large, pleading eyes stare out at the television audience. Her cheeks are sunken, her lips are drawn into an expression of pain. This four-year-old girl has not had food for days.

As the television camera pulls back from the child, it pans the enormous crowd behind her at an Ethiopian relief station. Thousands of people streamed to these camps in search of food. The camera, focusing in on several individuals, reveals the great variety of people gathered there. There are children of all ages, men and women from every walk of life.

Despite the variety, however, the viewer recognizes in all of them the face of the four-year-old girl, the pleading eyes, the anguished expression. It is the face of hunger, and one can almost feel its pain. While these scenes fill the screen, one hears the words of a popular song in the background: "We are the world, we are the children."

TV advertisements such as this were aired frequently during the Christmas season of 1984. In glaring contrast to the typical Christmas ads selling expensive electronic gadgets and the latest styles in clothes, these ads brought the Ethiopian famine and the plight of millions of starving people to public attention. They

## Ethiopian Famine in History

**3000 B.C.**
Abyssinia, later called Ethiopia, becomes the first African nation

**900 B.C.**
Menelik, son of Israel's King Solomon and the queen of Sheba, becomes first king of Ethiopia

**341 A.D.**
Christianity comes to Ethiopia

**1530**
Portuguese troops help Ethiopians defeat invading Somalis

**1845**
Irish potato famine begins

**1876**
Great famine of China

**1889**
Addis Ababa becomes Ethiopia's capital

**1896**
Emperor Menelik II turns back Italian invasion

**1900**
One hundred thousand Ethiopians die from a devastating drought

**1914**
World War I begins

**1921**
Great famine of Russia

**1930**
Emperor Haile Selassie I is crowned; establishes parliament

**1935**
Fascist Italy invades and conquers Ethiopia

**1939**
World War II begins

**1941**
British drive out Italians; Haile Selassie returns to throne

shocked the American public and persuaded many to open their hearts to a more genuine spirit of giving.

Soon millions of dollars in aid were pouring into Ethiopia. This aid saved many lives, but it came too late to avert one of the greatest tragedies of the twentieth century. From 1983 to 1986, 1.5 million Ethiopians died of starvation. That was the culmination of nearly two decades of famine that claimed more than seven million lives.

Ethiopia was not the only African country to suffer from famine during these two decades. From 1970 through 1987, all of northeastern Africa had experienced regular periods of drought. In the neighboring countries of Sudan, Chad, Somalia, and Yemen, famine also claimed millions of lives. Between the periods of drought in these countries, however, farmers were able to produce adequate crops to relieve some of the hunger and starvation. They even managed to store grains in case another drought came. When drought did return, these countries were not spared, but they were better prepared than Ethiopia.

In Ethiopia, other factors prevented the people from preparing for the inevitable droughts. In fact, these factors worked together with the drought conditions to make the situation even worse. As a result, Ethiopia did not just experience periods of famine between 1970 and 1987 like its neighbors. Instead, it suffered from two decades of uninterrupted famine.

What happened in Ethiopia resulted from a disastrous combination of land abuse, overpopulation, political turmoil, and dry weather. How these factors all converged to decide the tragic fate of this country and millions of its citizens is the subject of this book. To understand the full impact of that fate, we must look back to the early 1970s, when the various factors began to weave the tragic tale of the Ethiopian famine.

**1945**
Ethiopia becomes charter member of United Nations

**1962**
Eritrea becomes part of Ethiopia

**1970-1973**
Three million Ethiopians die of famine

**1974**
Army coup d'etat deposes Selassie; establishes Dergue government

**1977**
Civil war known as the Red Terror erupts in Ethiopia

**1984**
"Live-Aid" concert staged for Ethiopian famine relief

**1985**
Ethiopian famine reaches peak; is finally relieved by rain

**1987**
Lowest rainfall in a century causes another famine

**1989**
Attempted coup to topple Mengistu fails

**1990**
World Bank names Ethiopia world's poorest country

# One

# Before the Revolution

The village of Wardina is situated on a highland plateau in the province of Tigre, in northern Ethiopia. To the south and east, rugged mountains rise steeply overhead. To the north and west stretches the vast Arabian Desert. In the mountains west of Wardina, forty to forty-five inches of rain falls every year. This rain fills the mountain lakes and streams with ample water year round. There is probably enough water in these lakes and streams to irrigate all the farms in Ethiopia. But the mountains are too rugged to permit anyone to build pipelines from the mountain lakes to the plateaus below.

Normally, the additional water is not needed on the plateau around Wardina. The rainfall here is normally about twenty inches per year, and temperatures range from about sixty to eighty-five degrees Fahrenheit. This is perfect weather for growing grains, fruits, and vegetables of all kinds.

The lowland deserts that begin about eighty miles west of the village are quite different. Few people live in the desert, where temperatures often soar above 110° and less than seven inches of rain falls each year. Nomads, or wandering tribes of people who herd their cattle across the desert, are the only signs of life ever seen in the desert.

Wardina and the surrounding villages are inhabited by the Gurage tribe. This is one of seventy different tribes that make up the nation of Ethiopia. The people of Ethiopia can trace their history back more than five thousand years to the time when this small, independent nation on the northeastern coast of Africa, in an area known as the Horn, was called Abyssinia. That makes it the oldest nation on the entire African continent. Unlike every other African nation, Ethiopia was never colonized by any Middle Eastern or European power. Throughout history, it has remained an independent country. And until 1974, it was ruled by a line of emperors and empresses whose ancestors could be traced back to the biblical days of King Solomon. The last emperor was Haile Selassie, who ruled Ethiopia from 1930 until 1974.

About 90 percent of the people in Ethiopia live in rural villages, where they farm the land in much the same way as their ancestors did

About 90 percent of Ethiopians lived in rural villages and farmed the land using many of the same methods as their ancestors did.

for hundreds of years. They cultivate fields of wheat, barley, peas, beans, pumpkins, coffee, and false banana plants. Until 1974, most of the people followed traditional tribal laws and customs.

According to these customs, most people could not own land. That right was reserved for a small minority of tribal elders. The elders belonged to noble families whose ancestors had possessed the land for generations. All the other villagers were sharecroppers, or peasants who farmed the land owned by the nobility. In return for their work, the peasants were allowed to keep for themselves a certain portion of the crops they harvested. All the rest went to the landlords.

Most rural villagers lived in tradi-tional village homes, or *tukuls*, which are large, round, cone-shaped huts made from a mixture of tall grass and mud. The pointed roofs of these huts were made of long, dry reeds. The largest *tukuls* in the village belonged to the tribal elders, who were the wealthy landlords.

One reason the houses of the elders had to be large was so that they could house the many oxen they owned. At night, all the oxen were herded into the elder's house. The elders did not want to leave their oxen outside because hyenas came down to the village every night to scavenge for food. Any villagers who owned oxen, chickens, goats, or other livestock brought their animals indoors for the night.

The elders' houses also had to be

Most villagers lived in large, cone-shaped huts fashioned from tall grass and mud.

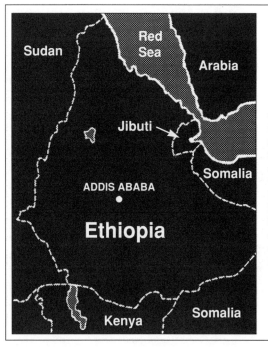

Ethiopia is located on the east coast of Africa, in the region commonly called the sub-Sahara. Lying just north of the equator, this ancient land is approximately the size of Texas and California combined. On its northeastern border is the Red Sea. In the first century A.D., Ethiopia's access to this busy waterway helped make it a great military and trading power. To the south and east lies the country of Somalia, while Kenya and Sudan make up its southern and western borders.

big because the men of the village often gathered there. They would meet in the *kakat*, a special room reserved for the head of the family and his guests. The elders sat on wooden stools, while the others sat below them on straw mats. They would discuss issues of importance to the village. The share of crops to be paid by the peasants as rent was set at these meetings, as were such things as marrying fees—the payment a man had to make to a girl's parents for the right to marry her. If one villager claimed that another had stolen something, or had done something else against tribal law, that case would also be heard at a gathering of the elders.

Until 1974, traditional life in the villages of Ethiopia went on as it had for centuries with little change.

Only the cycle of planting and harvesting and the ebb and flow of Ethiopia's two seasons—the rainy season, or *kremt*, and the dry season, or *bega*—brought variety to village life. The people made their tools, worked their land, and harvested their crops in much the same way as their ancestors had before them.

Most men and women still wore the traditional clothing. The common garment for both was called a *shamma*, and it was a loose, rectangular cotton shawl worn over the shoulders and arms. The *shamma* was worn loosely so that it could even be pulled over one's head to provide instant shade in the hot sun.

Men often wore cotton shirts and white pants under the *shamma*, while women usually wore a white cotton gown called a *k'amis*. Most

Ethiopian men, women, and children also wore lots of jewelry, especially beaded necklaces and bracelets.

Almost all villagers began their days early, rising to feed the cattle and chickens. Then the men, hitching their crude, handmade plows to mules, guided the plows through the hard clay-like soil. By hand, they planted seeds for wheat, barley, peas, beans, and pumpkins. They also tended their false banana plants. These plants with long, fan-shaped leaves were an important part of traditional village life. The Ethiopian people used the fibers of the leaves to weave baskets and pouches. The pulp inside the stems and roots was pounded into a kind of paste that was used for making a special bread, called *wusa* bread.

## Beef or Chicken a Luxury

Breads were a main part of the Ethiopian diet, especially in rural areas. Besides *wusa* bread, the Ethiopians made something like a pancake, which they called *injera*. *Injera* could be made with a variety of different grains, and it was often eaten with a spicy vegetable stew, or *wat*. On occasion, people added beef or chicken to their stew, but that was considered a luxury.

Every summer, everyone worked together to harvest the false banana plants. First, the men stripped the tall leaves from the plants and spread them on the ground to dry. Then, they pulled the trunks from the ground. Boys helped their fathers by carrying the trunks to shady groves, where the women and girls of the village pounded and scraped the roots and pulp to make the flour for *wusa* bread.

## Songs Taught Values

As the women worked, they often sang together. Their customary songs taught the values that were important in Ethiopian village life. One of their songs went like this:

*Wives of hard workers rejoice!*
*Your men planted hundreds of*
  *seedlings!*
*Luckless wife of a lazy man, what*
  *will you give your crying children?*
*Wives of hard workers rejoice!*
*You have nothing to worry about.*
*Wife of a lazy man, dress and be up!*
*You must go to market and buy*
  *cheap!*
*Wives of hard workers rejoice!*
*You are mothers to village orphans!*
*Wife of a lazy man, you have no rest!*
*Both summer and winter you look for*
  *bread.*
*Oh hard-working men, may no fire*
  *see your hands, nor any evil!*
*Oh lazy men, find wisdom and spirit*
  *to labor!*

In the traditional village, a woman's life was very different from a man's. Girls were taught to follow in their mothers' footsteps, tending to the home and vegetable garden, collecting water in large ceramic jars, preparing food, and caring for their younger brothers and sisters. If a village were lucky enough to have a school, girls rarely were allowed to attend.

The children began helping their

parents at home or in the fields when they were about six years old. At this young age, most village children already knew what was going to be expected of them as adults. The boys would grow up to be farmers, and the girls would become wives and have children.

## Children Were Greatly Valued

Since children were useful for helping with farming and domestic chores, they were greatly valued. In fact, the Ethiopians counted their wealth by such things as how many children they had, how many cattle they owned, and how big their houses were. Most women believed that the greatest contribution they could make to the family was to have lots of children.

In 1974, most of the people living in the rural villages of Ethiopia still believed that they should have large families. Yet the population throughout the country was growing so fast that it was becoming more and more difficult to feed all the children. The northern plateaus were especially overcrowded. As a result, many Ethiopian children died while still infants from illness and fever that their weak, undernourished bodies could not fight off.

Efforts to produce more food were not very successful. If anything, the farmland in northern Ethiopia was less productive than it had been hundreds of years ago. That is because most farmers in this region had not been taught modern farming methods. They still did things the way their ancestors had hundreds of years ago.

Year after year farmers planted the same crops in the same fields. Gradually, this method robbed the soil of valuable nutrients as the crops absorbed all that were available. Few farmers used fertilizers to put nutrients back into their soil. And because the demand for food continued to increase, they could not afford to let any of the land lie fallow and replenish itself.

As a matter of fact, Ethiopians continued to clear away the trees and wild grasses from acre after acre of forests and meadows so they could turn them into farmland. This had been going on for hundreds of years. Long ago, lush, green forests covered about half of Ethiopia's land. Since the 1600s, however, the people of Ethiopia have been clearing these forests.

In the short term, this seemed like an ideal solution, but the people did not realize that they were permanently altering the landscape, and they did not understand what they were doing to their environment. By 1970, only 7 percent of Ethiopia's land was still covered with trees.

## Trees and Grasses Are Critical

Both trees and wild grasses are critical to the ecology of the land. Trees help build up moisture in the atmosphere, which causes rain clouds to form. They also provide shade, which helps cool the land. In the hot, dry areas where there is no shade, the sun bakes the soil into a

An Ethiopian farmer slowly plows a rocky field with the help of two oxen. Erosion, deforestation and overgrazing of livestock have transformed semiarid land into desert that cannot be farmed.

hard crust. This makes the land unsuitable for farming. Rainwater that falls on the hard ground just runs off or evaporates instead of soaking in.

This dry soil is easily eroded, or carried away by wind and rain. For example, the landscape in northern Ethiopia has been scarred by gullies where heavy rains have washed the dirt away. When it rains, the eroded soil is carried into the nearest rivers and streams. Most of Ethiopia's rivers eventually dump into the Nile, and the silt, or eroded soil, is deposited on the Nile Delta in Egypt.

Just as deforestation exposes the soil to erosion, so does overgrazing. For centuries, farmers and nomadic herdsmen allowed their cows, sheep, oxen, and camels to graze at will throughout Ethiopia. Slowly, these animals removed the natural grasses and shrubbery that kept the soil from eroding.

The first areas affected by erosion and deforestation were the semiarid regions that lie between the deserts and the plateaus. Historically, these regions of Ethiopia had light rainfall, but enough to support farming. Gradually, however, the loss of trees, grasses, and topsoil made much of this land unproductive. Over the years, average rainfall in these regions has declined. Much of the land in Ethiopia that was once semiarid is now desert. The Ethiopians are no longer able to farm on these lands.

Even more devastating, perhaps, were the effects of erosion and deforestation on the fertile plateaus

Livestock have grazed the same land for centuries, removing the natural grasses and shrubbery that prevented erosion of topsoil.

where the majority of Ethiopians lived. Although the averages of temperature and rainfall in this area are quite moderate, the weather seems to follow a fifty-year cycle of unusually dry periods, wet periods, and moderate periods. About every fifty years, then, the plateaus of Ethiopia experience unusually dry weather, or drought. The water in the lakes and rivers evaporates quickly. Lakes become several feet shallower, and many riverbeds dry up completely. Wild grasses turn brown, and the sandy soil swirls in the hot wind. Crops wither and die.

Sometimes, these droughts last for several years. Because they cannot grow crops on the dry land, the people in the villages have little food to eat. If a drought goes on long enough, it may cause many people to starve to death. Before 1970, the last serious drought had occurred around 1900, when about 100,000 people in Ethiopia died of starvation.

Around 1970, another serious drought began in Ethiopia. Soon, the hot, dry weather combined with poor soil conditions and deforestation to turn the normally moderate plateaus into semiarid lands where few crops would grow. In many villages the elders rationed food supplies. No one had very much to eat, but most people had enough to survive. Still, the inadequate diet meant people became ill with flu, pneumonia, and other diseases. Especially infants, young children, and the elderly were too weak to fight off these diseases. Throughout Ethiopia the death toll from the drought began to rise and people looked to their emperor, Haile Selassie, for help.

# Two

# The Fall of an Empire

For centuries, Ethiopia had been ruled by an emperor. Like a king, an emperor is the supreme ruler of his empire and is the highest-ranking member of his country's aristocracy. When the emperor dies, the title is passed down to his chosen successor, usually the oldest son.

In Ethiopia, this method of passing on power was exercised not only by the emperor but by the rest of the country as well. This is because Ethiopia had a system of government known as feudalism. In a feudal society, only the aristocracy, or a select group of wealthy and influential families, is allowed to own land and hold political power. This right is passed down from father to son, from generation to generation.

A feudal society is relatively rare in current times. Today, most countries that once had a feudal society in their history have long since abandoned it. Historically, masses of people have risen up against the few people with power and replaced feudalism with a system of government in which the average person has more power and influence. In Ethiopia, however, the country remained primitive and unchanged, and democracy was never established. Its hot deserts and inaccessible mountains divided people into small, isolated tribes. These tribes did not know of any other lifestyle—they lived the way their ancestors had always lived.

Rural villagers, who made up 90 percent of Ethiopia's population, also maintained the ancient, traditional ways of life. But in the cities, Western influence had begun to erode the feudal society by the end of the 1800s. In 1889, emperor Menelik II established Addis Ababa as the nation's capital. Menelik brought in European architects to design palaces and public buildings in a contemporary style. This modernization drew international banks and businesses, which brought new wealth into the city. By 1930, Addis Ababa was a modern city with more than one million residents. Cars, trucks, and buses filled its streets, while high-rise offices, apartment buildings, and homes formed its new skyline. This bustling, Western-style metropolis attracted businesspeople and workers from every corner of Africa.

But beyond the bright lights of its international business and enter-

Addis Ababa, Ethiopia's capital city, is a mix of bustling streets, modern
high-rise office  buildings, and business and entertainment districts. It
also is home to hundreds of thousands of impoverished villagers who come
to the city seeking riches.

tainment districts, Addis Ababa housed hundreds of thousands of the poorest people in all of Africa. Many of them had come to the city because they had heard rumors about its riches. Few were prepared, however, for what they found there. Everything in the city was new and different, and the kinds of skills they needed to succeed were unfamiliar to these poor villagers. Few could read or write, and even fewer possessed technical knowledge or business sense. Soon, their hopes of riches were replaced with desperate pleas for money or food.

## A New Emperor

In 1930, the nation of Ethiopia crowned a new emperor, Haile Selassie, who approved of the modern industry and technology that were changing his country. Yet Selassie did not want to give up his power as emperor. Selassie tried to strike a balance between modernizing the economy and modernizing the government. He appealed to the governments of the United States and Western Europe to assist in improving the country's schools, hospitals, roads, and transportation systems. He also took steps to introduce some aspects of a democratic government, while maintaining his own position as emperor.

Selassie approved a democratic constitution and gave citizens the right to elect representatives to a national parliament. Yet, he declared himself emperor for life, with absolute power over the parliament. Selassie's plan was to have the par-

liamentary government take over after his death.

This worked for a while, but by the 1960s, many of the students educated at the schools and universities Selassie helped build challenged his authority. They rejected Selassie's parliamentary government. They wanted Selassie to resign so they could establish a communist government to take his place. One of the goals of communism is to redistribute land by taking it away from large landholders and giving it to all the people.

By 1970, the most powerful student rebel group was called the Dergue. Its leader, Mengistu Haile Mariam, successfully appealed to the Soviet Union for weapons to help carry out an armed struggle against the government of Haile Selassie. In the midst of this struggle,

Haile Selassie was Ethiopia's emperor from 1930 until his overthrow in 1974.

Mengistu Haile Mariam led the rebellion that brought down the Selassie government.

a serious famine was spreading across the countryside. The Dergue blamed deaths from starvation on the selfishness and greed of the wealthy landowners.

Aware of the worsening famine, Selassie could have asked the United States and Western Europe for more aid. But he did not. Many experts believe he did not want to reveal what desperate trouble his people were in. So, while the rest of the world remained ignorant of Ethiopia's plight, more than three million Ethiopians died of starvation between 1970 and 1973.

By 1974, thousands more were on the verge of starvation. The drought continued, and Selassie still did not ask for foreign aid. His stubbornness cost him the support of his people. Everywhere, people called for his resignation.

In September 1974, the Dergue was able to persuade key figures in the government army to turn against Selassie. This group took command of the military and arrested Selassie as a traitor to his own country.

As he was taken from the palace, crowds of people gathered outside to cheer his overthrow. They laughed and jeered at their former emperor as he was driven away to prison in an old, battered Volkswagen. A few months later, Selassie died in prison.

At first, the majority of Ethiopians welcomed Selassie's overthrow and the military takeover. The military supported Mengistu's Dergue party, which took control of the government. The Dergue disbanded the Ethiopian parliament and abolished the constitution. It promised new elections as soon as the structure for a "true democracy of the people" could be put into place. Until then, the Dergue assumed total control of the government.

## Strip Land from the Wealthy

The party instantly won the support of most Ethiopians by seeking international assistance for victims of the famine. It gained even more ardent support among rural peasants by issuing its first land reform measure. This measure outlawed any private citizen from owning more than ten hectares of land. It also made it illegal for one person to hire another to work on a farm. The goal of the land reform was to strip the land from the wealthy landowners and redistribute it among the peasants.

As soon as they learned about this, most peasants were willing to do whatever the Dergue asked of them. That included joining local peasant associations, which were official organizations of the Dergue party. In fact, joining a peasant association was a requirement for receiving ten free hectares of land from the government. In this way, the Dergue dramatically built its membership in the countryside.

There were also certain requirements for membership in a peasant association. Members were expected to attend all rallies and meetings supporting the Dergue. All family members had to attend literacy classes, where they learned to read and write. Part of their education included learning to read stories about capitalist villains and

peasant heroes. The association leaders taught them that the greedy landlords were responsible for the food shortages the nation was then suffering.

The Dergue wanted the peasants to turn against the tribal leaders who owned the land in the villages. The Dergue gave members of the peasant associations weapons and training and authorized them to use force to take land away from former tribal leaders if they resisted.

In the cities, the Dergue led a similar movement against private business owners. It took control of all banks, newspapers, broadcasting companies, hospitals, and many other private businesses. To receive jobs in these nationalized companies, individuals were required to join neighborhood associations. These were similar to the peasant associations. Members were required to attend literacy classes, meetings, and rallies. Many of them were required to join the militia to keep peace in the cities.

## Confusion Reigned

By 1977, the drought that had plagued Ethiopia came to an end. As rain fell in abundance and farmers turned their attention to producing a good harvest, the Dergue faced its first serious challenges. Its massive overhaul of the economy was still incomplete. In cities and villages, confusion reigned. Some landlords had been evicted from their farms while their crops were waiting to be harvested. Other land-

Thousands of Ethiopians gather in Addis Ababa to commemorate the tenth anniversary of the 1974 overthrow of Emperor Haile Selassie.

lords had not even planted their fields. Many peasants turned land-owners did not have the skills to farm without the direction of the former tribal leaders. They were not sure what to plant or when to plant it. This meant that even though there was enough rainfall, there was still a shortage of food.

Out of frustration, some peasants turned back to their former leaders—landlords and tribal elders—for leadership. In Eritrea and Ogaden, many of these leaders formed resistance movements. They wanted their provinces to declare their independence from the Ethiopian government.

In the cities, everything was just as chaotic. The government appointed new managers for the factories, banks, and stores it had taken over. Many of these managers were given their jobs as a reward for loyalty, not because they were trained to run the businesses. The change from a free economy to a state-controlled economy left most businesses in disorder or complete ruin.

Many Ethiopians began to wonder whether the new government was any better than the old one. Critics spoke against its mismanagement of the economy. Even other communist organizations challenged the Dergue, claiming that its leaders were incompetent. The largest of these organizations, the People's Revolutionary Movement, began staging guerrilla attacks on government-owned farms, businesses, and factories.

In the face of mounting opposition, Mengistu knew that his party had little chance of keeping power if it held free elections. Instead, Mengistu tightened his grip on the country through the use of force.

During 1977 and 1978, Mengistu ordered his army and militia to attack every group that he perceived as an opponent to his continued rule. This included the secessionist movements in Eritrea and Ogaden, the People's Revolutionary Movement, student and faculty organizations in the universities, former business leaders in the cities, and tribal leaders in the countryside. For two years, Ethiopia was in a state of civil war, which the people now refer to as the Red Terror.

Thousands were killed in clashes with the government. People suspected of being subversives were ambushed and murdered by government death squads. In Addis Ababa, the victims of these ambushes were often left lying in the streets as a warning to others who might be thinking of opposing the Dergue.

Mengistu's Red Terror crushed the organized opposition to his rule. At the same time, however, it dashed the hopes of many Ethiopians who thought Selassie might be replaced with a better system of government. As the 1970s came to a close, the nation fell deeper and deeper into poverty. Its factories did not manufacture, its farms did not produce, and its people did not stay. From 1976 to 1980, more than two million Ethiopians, from a total population of about forty-five million, fled into neighboring countries.

# Three

# In Search of Food: A Nation of Nomads

Between 1974 and 1980, Mengistu Haile Mariam and his government put the theories of communism to work in Ethiopia, trying to reverse the nation's misfortunes. With rebellion in the cities, secessionist movements in the country, and waning loyalty within the party, Ethiopia fell deeper and deeper into poverty and chaos. Even though the drought had ended around 1976, the new farm owners could not keep up with the demand for food.

That prompted the government to try new methods of increasing food production. It enacted a new land reform program that was far more drastic than the first one. This plan called for two extreme measures: resettlement and collective farming. The resettlement program was meant to move farmers from overpopulated and overcultivated farmlands in northern Ethiopia to fertile, undeveloped land in central and southern Ethiopia. And instead of being given small farms of their own, farmers were put to work on state-owned and -operated collective farms.

The theory behind resettlement was logical. The northern farmlands were indeed overcultivated and overpopulated. They no longer produced as much as they once had. Therefore, relocating people from the north to the south, which had more land and fewer people, seemed practical. However, most of the proposed new farmland in the south was heavily forested or covered with wild grasses. Powerful tractors and trucks were needed to help clear this land. At first, the Dergue would need money to make its resettlement program work. But it predicted that the new farms in the south would quickly begin to produce food and the nation would solve its food shortage problem once and for all. When the Mengistu government asked the United Nations for funds to help with the resettlement program, its request was approved.

At first, the resettlement program was strictly voluntary. As an incentive to relocate, the government promised every volunteer family a house, free land, farm tools, oxen, and seed to plant. The government made films showing the volunteers what their new homes would look

Thousands of Ethiopian farmers voluntarily resettled in the south to farm. Only after they arrived did many learn that the land would be owned by the government and the harvest shared by many.

like. They depicted modern-looking frame houses, row upon row of tall, thick stands of grain ready to harvest, and villages with modern schools and medical clinics.

## An Offer Too Good to Refuse

For families on the brink of starvation and living in run-down, disorderly villages, resettlement was too good an offer to refuse. Although it often meant leaving the village where their ancestors had lived for centuries and giving up the only homes they had ever known, thousands of Ethiopian farmers volunteered for resettlement.

When these volunteers arrived at the resettlement sites, however, they often found that the land they were supposed to farm was still covered with trees and wild grass. No farm sites had been cleared. And they were informed that their new houses, schools, and hospitals had not yet been built. So the first job for most settlers was building the houses and other facilities that had been promised to them.

As the settlers soon discovered, everything at the resettlement sites was controlled by government officials. Instead of individual homes, they were required to build large, crude barracks. As many as fifty families, or about two hundred people, were crowded into a single barracks about seventy-five feet long.

After the barracks were built, the settlers were required to begin work on building single-family homes. In a typical resettlement site, however, only a dozen or so of these homes were ever built. And they were occupied by the families of the government officials who managed the resettlement projects. The other volunteer settlers were required to remain in the barracks permanently —a far cry from the new homes they had envisioned when they first volunteered.

Most volunteers for resettlement were also unaware that they had become part of the government's new collective farming experiment. Under this program, no peasant owned his own land. The farms belonged to the government, and the farmers were expected to work together to make these farms productive. Then they would share the harvest or any money that came from selling part of their harvest.

## Worse Off than Before

To many peasants, this new system seemed no different from the old landlord system, except that the state was their landlord. In many ways they were even worse off than before. At least under the old system, they were allowed to farm a piece of land for themselves. Often, the resettlement projects required so much work to clear the land, build barracks and other buildings, and fulfill other peasant association responsibilities, that no crops were even planted for the first two or three years.

The collective farm program was not reserved for resettlement areas. After 1982, the government began to implement it throughout the country. Land that had been taken

from wealthy landowners and redistributed to the peasants was now turned into government-owned collectives. Land left behind by peasants who had volunteered for resettlement, or by those who had gone searching for food, was also turned into collective farms.

Despite the government's efforts, these farms did not prosper. The farmers had little incentive to work hard. When their crops were harvested, the state collected and distributed them however it saw fit. As one farmer told a reporter: "There are farmers in our area who can produce in one harvest enough for seven years. But no more. This is not because the land has changed but because the government takes it all."

The idea behind the collective

farm was that the farmers would share the harvest or the profits equally. But it never seemed to work that way. The peasants who stayed on their land were told that their crops were needed to feed the resettlement volunteers, or the soldiers in the army, or someone else. The government left barely enough food for the farmers' families to survive. One peasant on a collective farm complained about the Dergue officials who ran their farm: "They are taking our grain, our money, and our people."

Neither collective farming nor resettlement was working the way the government had planned. In 1982, out of desperation, millions of impoverished citizens packed their belongings and left their homes in search of food. There were already food shortages, and millions of impoverished people were living on the brink of starvation. Many parts of Ethiopia, especially on the northern plateaus, had experienced dry weather that year. Another drought would push the nation over the brink, hurtling it toward one of the worst famines in world history. The next year was another dry year.

By 1984, famine had reached disaster proportions. In response, the Dergue sought foreign help. In November 1984, government officials took foreign reporters into the countryside. What the reporters saw and photographed there shocked the world. The extent of hunger,

Crops could no longer grow and people could not survive on this parched, cracked Ethiopian earth—a result of government mismanagement and several years of drought.

## WHILE MILLIONS STARVED, FOOD ROTTED ON DOCKS

Distributing food to the hungry in the outlying regions of Ethiopia was a problem, not only because the country lacked trucks and roads, but because the government was busy using its trucks for other purposes. Most of them were being used to transport peasants as part of the massive resettlement program. Even trucks that had been donated by foreign governments for transporting food were used for transporting resettlement volunteers. By the middle of 1985, when a plentiful supply of grain was being unloaded at the port of Aseb, most of it rotted on the dock because there were no trucks to haul it to mills or storage elevators.

31

poverty, and disease was worse than anyone had imagined.

Reports estimated that more than half a million people had died of starvation in 1984. Many were young children. Newsmagazines and television broadcasts showed throngs of Ethiopian people traveling from village to village in search of food. Their scrawny arms and legs revealed how long it had been since they last ate. Etched on their ghost-like faces was a resignation to constant pain and hunger.

Pictures of dying babies and row upon row of fly-covered corpses stunned the civilized world. When British Prime Minister Margaret Thatcher and Australian Prime Minister Robert Hawke first saw these pictures, they were reported to have broken into tears. Overnight, Western governments began pouring money and supplies into Ethiopia at record-breaking rates.

U.S. President Ronald Reagan and the leaders of other Western governments had been reluctant to

A starving child cries at a feeding center in a Southern Ethiopian village. Some estimates said more than half a million people died of starvation in 1984.

European and American entertainers performed to raise money to aid Ethiopia. These entertainers took part in the American effort, called USA for Africa.

help Ethiopia because of its communist government and its ties to the Soviet Union. But when they realized how badly the Ethiopian people were suffering, they knew they had to help. West Germany sent more than $6 million worth of food to the Ethiopian government. Italy brought in construction teams to build hospitals, and Canada and Australia each contributed tens of thousands of tons of grain. The most generous nation of all was the United States. It contributed over $100 million in aid, supplying nearly one-third of Ethiopia's food for 1985.

Individuals and private organizations also pitched in to help the starving masses of Ethiopians. The largest contributions came from benefit concerts and recordings by international rock stars. In December 1984, a group of more than fifty rock musicians collaborated on the hit single "We Are the World," an emotional appeal to the people of the world to help those in need. Millions of dollars in proceeds from royalties and sales of the record were donated to the Ethiopian Relief Fund.

That organization was founded by Irish singer and songwriter Bob Geldof. Geldof also organized the popular Live Aid telethon concerts, televised simultaneously from London and New York. Hundreds of rock stars performed in these concerts, which generated more than ten million dollars in pledges to the Relief Fund. Geldof later made several trips to Ethiopia himself to supervise the distribution of food provided by his organization.

As Geldof and thousands of other Westerners soon discovered, getting food to Ethiopia was only half of the problem. Once it was there, making sure it reached those who needed it most was a frustrating and often unsuccessful mission. Most of the starving people lived in the country, and there were few roads into the rugged Ethiopian countryside. For many villagers it was a two-day walk just to the nearest road. And there were only an estimated six hundred trucks in the entire country. Most of these were controlled by the Ethiopian government. Out of desperation, many peasants attempted to walk to the nearest roads, hoping to find trucks carrying food. But in their starving condition, thousands of these desperate nomads were killed by their efforts.

For foreign officials and volunteers, the greatest frustration of all was working with Mengistu and his government. Mengistu recognized that in a starving nation, food meant power. As long as the government could control the distribution of food, it could stay in power. So Mengistu used the food, medicine, and money donated by Western nations to advance his plans.

When the United States and

Because of a shortage of trucks, getting food to starving Ethiopians was difficult.

other Western governments began providing abundant aid to Ethiopia in 1984, the government used the promise of food to lure people into resettlement programs. Instead of taking food to the villages where people were starving, the government set up relief stations in the larger villages and market towns where people traditionally went to buy and sell goods. When they learned that relief stations had been set up there, people arrived at the market towns by the thousands.

## Difficult Choices

Even at the relief stations, there was not always enough food to go around. Workers at the stations sometimes had to make difficult choices about who should be fed first. Often, the government made the choice for them. It announced that food was available only for those willing to resettle in a new area.

Ahmed Mohammed, a former landlord who eventually fled to Sudan, was among those who sought help at one of the relief stations. He recalled that people of all ages and from all walks of life came in search of food: "The old and the sick came, children and youths and famine victims. Some very old people were even brought on camels. I carried my sick wife into town on a stretcher with the help of a neighbor. We were all full of expectations."

One thing they were not expecting was to be taken prisoner. But according to Ahmed, that is exactly what happened to many of the people seeking food. "At the assembly centers the peasants were rounded up by soldiers and militia men. . . . During these operations anyone in town looking like a peasant—the Koran student who was in the marketplace, a young man who wanted to visit his mother, a peasant selling grain, a young man selling wood— was captured and resettled," he said.

The government used other ploys as well. For example, it issued a requirement that all peasants in a particular area bring their oxen to the nearest village for vaccination. When the peasants showed up, their oxen were confiscated and the peasants locked up in "holding camps" from which they would be assigned a resettlement location.

## Little Humanitarian Concern

On other occasions, the militia or peasant associations in an area were assigned a quota of volunteers to organize for resettlement. How the quota was reached was left entirely to the militia or association members. As reported by Peter Niggli, a Swiss relief official who observed these activities firsthand, the methods employed by the militia showed little humanitarian concern. "Villages are enclosed by militias at night or in the early morning hours, and all inhabitants the troops can get hold of are rounded up. The people are told the lie that they will be brought to a political assembly in the nearest town," Niggli reported.

The troops caught the candidates

for resettlement asleep, sick in bed, or while harvesting, ploughing, threshing, herding cattle, repairing a fence, or just passing through. They showed no regard for keeping families together. Indeed, the government seemed to have a preference for separating children from their parents. That way they could raise the children in state-run orphanages and educate them in the virtues of communism. Although exact figures of how many families were divided by the resettlement program are unavailable, a comment by a peasant who managed to flee from one of the holding camps is typical: "Everything occurs, but not a complete family: men without their family (the majority of cases); men with one child; women with some of their children but never with all of them; children with no parents, women with no husband or children. And it made no difference whether someone was ill or not, or whether a woman was pregnant or not."

The holding camps were nothing more than prison camps, where the resettlement "volunteers" were kept like common criminals for weeks at a time. Food shortages were frequent in the holding camps, and what food people did get was meager. Sometimes, they went days without a meal. Several thousand resettlement candidates died in these camps. Those who survived were sent to resettlement sites where they were not much better off.

Anger spread throughout Ethiopia, but it was greatest in the provinces of Eritrea and Ogaden, where the majority of citizens favored declaring their independence from

Government officials lured people into resettlement programs by taking food meant for starving villagers to market towns and offering it to those who agreed to relocate.

Ethiopia. To put down violent uprisings in these provinces, the government concentrated its resettlement efforts on those it considered its enemies. Its aim was to weaken the opposition by dividing it.

In the province of Ogaden, for example, the government designated large areas of land for its resettlement and collective farming programs. Then, it filled these farms almost entirely with peasants from the northern province of Tigre. When rebel Oromos, the largest ethnic group in Ethiopia, took out their hostility by attacking the collective farms, the government supplied the Tigrean workers with rifles to defend themselves. As a result, the Tigreans replaced the government as the object of the Oromos' hatred, and the secessionist movement in Ogaden was overshadowed by the ethnic conflict between Tigreans and Oromos.

Eritrea was also targeted for massive resettlement programs. Between the resettlement activity and the continued drought, the leaders of the rebel movements were unable to find many people to join their ranks.

In most cases, resettlement, which was supposed to be the government's answer to famine, actually made the famine worse. Some farmers were forced from their land, even though they had fields of wheat ready for harvest. The wheat then rotted in the fields. Other farmers did not bother to plant their crops because they knew they would not be around to harvest them.

Harvested crops were confiscated by the government for distribution. But the government placed a higher priority on resettlement than on food distribution, and sometimes, while thousands of people were dying of starvation daily, the government allowed piles of grain and other food to rot in warehouses and on loading docks.

Yet in September 1984, exactly ten years after the overthrow of Haile Selassie, the Dergue sponsored a huge, nationwide festival celebrating the tenth anniversary of its takeover. In Addis Ababa there were fireworks, parades, and visits from foreign dignitaries. There was free food, beer, and wine, and dancing in the streets that went on long into the night. The parades featured Ethiopian, Cuban, and North Korean marching soldiers. Processions of tanks and MIG jets given to Ethiopia by the Soviet Union displayed the military might of this starving nation.

For a nation that could not feed itself, it was an incredible display of excess. While infants in the countryside died because they had no milk, the Dergue spent over $100 million celebrating the tenth anniversary of its rise to power.

# Four

# Land of the Dead

By January 1985, the famine had reached its peak. Nationwide, the number of people living on the verge of starvation was estimated at eight million, about one out of every five Ethiopians. Nearly three million people had left their homes to wander in search of food. Thousands of famine victims streamed into temporary relief camps faster than the camps could supply food.

In the small town of Adigrat, on the border between Tigre and Eritrea, about ten thousand starving people huddled together inside a few tin sheds. Gray, ragged *shammas* hung limply over the scrawny arms and legs of the famine victims. Many of them had already lost more than half of their body weight. Their cheeks were sunken, making their eyes appear abnormally large. Mothers carried young children on their backs or crying infants cra-

dled in their arms. The children were only skin and bones, and some had swollen stomachs, a symptom of extreme malnutrition.

The doctors and nurses at the camp treated victims of pneumonia, influenza, dysentery, tuberculosis, typhoid, and blindness, all resulting from malnutrition. Among the victims, there were many who were beyond help. A nine-year-old boy carried his mother to the mission on his back. Within minutes after reaching the mission, she died in his arms.

The anguished screams of mothers whose children died of hunger, the wailing of children who could not find their parents, the crying of babies who just wanted to be fed, and the constant shouting of *"Tumini, tumini"* (I'm hungry, I'm hungry): this was the harsh, steady background noise at all the relief centers in Ethiopia.

Sister Marie McAuliffe, a relief worker at Adigrat, recalled her feeling of helplessness when she first arrived: "No TV coverage could capture what we felt when right off we saw a father carrying his dying daughter on his back, or when we saw a family scratching the earth for seeds, which is the last thing they do before they lie down and wait to die."

There were about twenty-five thousand victims at the refugee camp in Bati, a small town in the mountains of Tigre. The Bati camp looked like a war-ravaged battlefield. There were only enough temporary sheds to house the medical

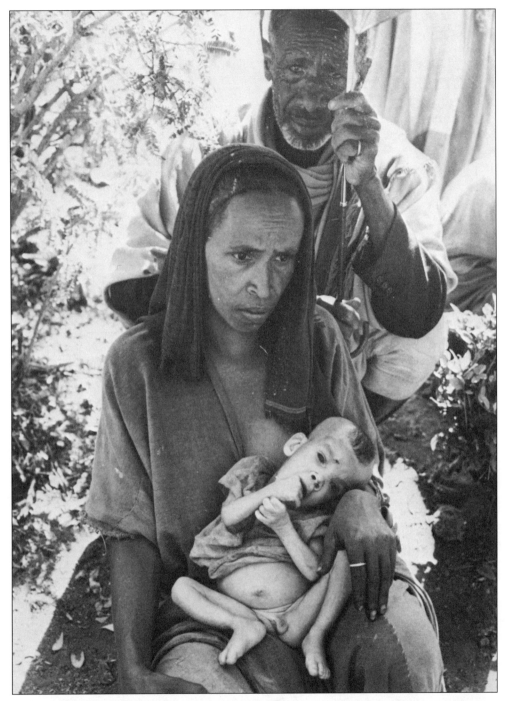

The famine's relentless grasp reached across the generations, squeezing the
life from entire families. By January 1985, eight million Ethiopian's were thought
to be on the verge of starvation.

unit. Several thousand patients were crammed into these buildings, but most of the refugees occupied foxholes dug in the hard, parched earth. The best-furnished foxholes had branches to cover them, lending shelter from the mountain breezes that blew especially cold at night.

The Bati camp was so overrun with victims that it could not give food or medical attention to everyone. Miles Harris, a British doctor, and his wife, Janet, a nurse, had come to Ethiopia to assist with the relief effort. Every morning, they faced the grim task of determining which people were in greatest need of medical help, which ones needed the most food, and which were beyond help. "You can tell who will live and who will die," Janet said. "The dying ones have no light left in their eyes."

Victims more likely to survive were grouped and identified with colored wristbands. Children who were 70 percent below normal weight were given pink bands. They were fed four times per day—a diet of bread, protein-enriched rice, water, and vitamin supplements. No fresh vegetables, fruits, or meats were available. Children who were just a little stronger were fed twice per day. They wore red wristbands.

The doors to the feeding sheds had to be closely guarded at all times against the crush of hungry people desperate to get inside. But even those scattered outside in the filthy, insect- and disease-ridden camp could consider themselves

---

**VOLUNTEER DOCTORS PROTESTING RESETTLEMENT PROGRAM WERE THROWN OUT**

Doctors Without Borders was one of the first international relief organizations to come to Ethiopia to help ease the famine crisis of the 1980s. Volunteers with this organization witnessed the intentional withholding of food and humanitarian aid from areas of Eritrea and Tigre that were held by rebels fighting against the government. Doctors Without Borders set up secret relief stations in these areas to help the hundreds of thousands of starving victims.

In December 1985, the organization was ordered out of Ethiopia by the Ethiopian government. According to organization members, armed militiamen burst into their camps, seized their equipment, confiscated their trucks, medicines, and food stores, and beat many of the volunteers. The government banned Doctors Without Borders from any further activity in Ethiopia, declaring the organization an "enemy of the revolution."

---

lucky. As Miles Harris pointed out, "The ones who make it to this camp are the strong ones. The other 80 percent are dying up in the hills, too weak to move."

There was another shed at the Bati camp, a wooden hut known in the Afar language as *zawya*. It means "house of the dead." Every day, hundreds of bodies were carried to the hut and laid on the earthen floor. Inside the house of the dead, Hussein Yussuf, a sixty-year-old man, helped prepare the bodies for makeshift funerals. As he washed the shriveled body of a three-year-old boy, Yussuf mused, "This is the first water this child has had for a long,

With the relief camp behind them and miles of dry, lifeless earth around them, camp residents remove the body of a famine victim for burial.

long time."

He wrapped the body in a filthy burlap shroud and laid it on a bed of fresh eucalyptus leaves alongside twenty-six other bodies. This was the four hundredth body of the week, he informed a reporter, "and the numbers keep going up." Some of the bodies were taken to a grave site and buried in common graves. Some parents carried their children's bodies to the Ethiopian Orthodox Church in the neighboring village. There, as priests under bright umbrellas chanted ageless prayers, the tiny bodies were placed in a long trench.

In Mekele, the capital of Tigre, the Don Bosco Technical High School was turned into a relief camp. The students at the school helped run the camp. Mulugeta Teare, one of these students, recalled his work at the camp and the awful conditions there: "I carried stones, built latrines, and buried the dead. There were so many people, and the whole area was stinking. Every day in the church we would wrap the bodies in cloth and pile them on top of each other, ready to be buried. But because I am small and not too strong, I could not lift as many as the others."

The experience of this fourteen-year-old boy, which was typical of many of Ethiopia's young people, made him mature beyond his years. He spoke with the tone and thoughtfulness of an adult who has experienced suffering firsthand and who has come to understand the suffering of others and the fragility of happiness. But Teare's worst experiences were not at the relief center in Mekele.

In the spring of 1985, Teare was permitted to leave the school and return to his village in Wardina. He had received word that his sixteen-year-old sister, Salamarit, had died of dysentery. Within days of her death, two more of his brothers died.

When he returned to his village, Teare found that it was only a ghost of its former self. It was the time of year to be planting, yet he saw little activity in the fields. On the roadway, he passed many of the villagers who were heading out of the village in search of food. Most of them were so thin and weak that they could barely walk. Still, Teare recognized their faces as the people he had seen almost every day of his life while growing up in the village.

A common funeral for his sister and two brothers was held at the mission church in the neighboring city, where Teare had started school seven years earlier. After the funeral, he knew that it was time to leave his village, permanently.

Looking back, Teare knew that the best thing for him to do was to bury his sorrows in his work. "I was helpless. After the funeral all I could do was come back to school and study. When I study hard, I forget," he said.

By June of 1985, Teare and his fellow students had resumed their normal studies. The crisis was far from over, but more aid was arriving from the United States and other countries. The church in Mekele had built a new medical

Whole villages were decimated by the famine. Many of those who could leave, did. The rest remained behind.

Through the efforts of foreign relief organizers, the Ethiopian government made more trucks available for food convoys.

clinic and relief center, so the students had gone back to school.

Around the country, the relief effort was slowly turning the tide against starvation and disease. As more Western supervisors came to Ethiopia to oversee the relief efforts, the government became more cooperative. Distribution channels opened up. Helicopters and small airplanes arrived to carry food into the hills where starving masses waited for it to arrive.

Food from the international agencies also began to arrive in larger quantities at the relief stations. The famine was not over, but the relief effort had made it change direction. Death rates were dropping. At Adrigrat, Sister McAuliffe began to notice changes, too. The many babies that the nurses had helped deliver gained, rather than lost, weight after their births. Relief workers were able to direct their attention to matters other than food. They sorted out donated clothing and began dressing the refugees in Western-style T-shirts.

Sister McAuliffe recalled an incident from the summer of 1985 that made the whole relief effort seem worthwhile. While sitting in her room in one of the temporary buildings, she saw through the window a bearded, barefoot old man in a

robe that was more holes than cloth. "He looked so hungry, that I gave him a slice of bread. After I finished I went outside, and there he was kneeling on the ground. Over and over he was thanking God. But when he saw me watching him, he came right over, very gracious, very dignified. He dropped down and began kissing my feet. I just stood there and cried," she said.

*Kremt,* the rainy season in Ethiopia, usually begins in June. And in June of 1985, the rain began to fall. It was the beginning of the first season of normal rainfall in about five years. The fields began to turn green with the first shoots of grain, corn, and vegetables. Although starvation was still far greater than acceptable levels, there was at least some hope, for the first time in years, that it was declining.

## Five

# "Why All This Suffering?"

From 1983 through 1985, 1.5 million Ethiopians died from the famine. When Sister Marie McAuliffe first arrived in Ethiopia in 1985, she was overwhelmed by what she found there. She was a devout Christian, but all the pain, agony, and suffering seemed so cruel that it led her to question her God. She ranted in prayer, "Why all this suffering? How can You let this happen? You must have a heart. Please, dear Lord, help them . . . and help me."

Despite the grief and anguish, thousands of volunteers like McAuliffe, from all around the world, found the strength and the will to come to the aid of the Ethiopian people. With their help and the financial assistance of millions of others, the famine was halted in 1985.

It had been one of the most devastating famines in history, but it could have been much worse. About five million Ethiopians were on the verge of starvation in 1984 when the relief effort was put into high gear. It is frightening to imagine how many more might have died without the intensive relief effort or without the rains that began to fall in June 1985.

As the immediate danger of starvation passed, however, it became clear that the famine had been worse in Ethiopia than in any of its neighboring countries that had experienced drought. From 1970 through 1984, all of northeastern Africa had experienced regular periods of drought. In the countries of Yemen, Sudan, and Chad, famine also claimed the lives of many thousands of people. Yet during the productive years between periods of drought, these countries recovered and prepared themselves for the next drought, just as farmers in Ethiopia had done traditionally. This periodic recovery helped to limit the disaster in these countries. But in Ethiopia a disastrous combination of weather, land abuse, overpopulation, and political turmoil produced nearly ten years of unceasing famine.

One of the reasons for the severity of the famine was the overcultivation and overgrazing found in Ethiopia. These practices led to soil depletion, deforestation, and erosion. As the population of Ethiopia continued to grow, the demand for food increased, worsening the con-

Ethiopian farmers overcultivated and overgrazed the land, severely depleting it of nutrients for growing much-needed crops.

dition of the land.

Some social scientists and economists say that this cycle of overcultivation, drought, and famine proves the validity of the Malthusian theory, which was formulated by the nineteenth-century English scientist Thomas Malthus. He theorized that the limited resources of the earth would not support an ever increasing population and that disease and starvation would halt population growth. He wrote, "The power of population is indefinitely greater than the power of the earth to provide all of man's needs."

In other words, when the population grows too large for the available resources of a region, famine and disease are nature's tools for bringing the population back into balance. According to Malthus, overpopulation is not a matter of too many people but of the lack of resources to feed, clothe, and shelter those people.

## Outdated, Inefficient System

In Ethiopia's case, overpopulation and the famine of the 1970s and 1980s were the result of an outdated and inefficient agricultural and economic system that could not keep up with the growing needs of the people. Without modern technology, food production could not increase. In fact, the Dergue came to power because Haile Selassie, the last emperor of Ethiopia, offered no solution to widespread famine and starvation. Even Selassie had recognized that Ethiopia had to be modernized. Naively, however, he be-

The nineteenth-century English scientist Thomas Malthus theorized that the earth's limited resources could not support a growing population.

lieved this could be done while holding on to the old-fashioned feudal order and to his position as emperor.

Selassie's overthrow and the demolition of the old aristocratic order were inevitable. The old order relied on outdated beliefs about who should be allowed to own land and who should prosper. It was supported by superstition and tradition. As soon as young people from the villages began to go to schools, they began to challenge the ancient superstitions and beliefs of their parents and their village elders. They learned how backward their country was in producing food and other goods and how outdated its system of government was.

Unfortunately, the Dergue government that took over in Ethiopia was at least as tyrannical as the Selassie government. This, too, fit a predictable social pattern that has occurred throughout the twentieth century. In countries like Russia, China, Nicaragua, Cuba, Vietnam, Korea, and Cambodia, aristocratic governments have suddenly been overthrown and then replaced by equally fanatic socialist governments.

That may be because people in these countries, unlike those of European heritage, did not have a strong tradition of democracy. In Europe, the transition from a feudal society to a democratic one happened slowly, over hundreds of years. In places like Ethiopia, where time had practically stood still for centuries, revolutionary leaders seemed determined to make their country catch up with the rest of the world instantly. The only way to do this was to force people to do things against their will and with little concern for their immediate well-being.

Revolutionary governments like the Dergue usually embrace communism because they believe it is the quickest way to achieve a revolution. They argue that violence and tyranny are sometimes necessary to persuade the uneducated masses to accept beneficial social change.

In Ethiopia, violence and tyranny and a serious drought made for a lethal combination. Members of the Dergue now claim that although this period of Ethiopian history was painful, everyone benefited from it.

It may be too soon to judge the communist revolution in Ethiopia,

Signs like this one sprouted in the capital after the revolution that overthrew Emperor Haile Selassie. The revolution's leaders initially won widespread support by promising a lot to people who had little.

but in its first decade, it forced the people of Ethiopia to endure the worst famine in its history. Although the weather, population, and environmental conditions all played a role, almost every refugee who fled from Ethiopia during the famine blames the suffering entirely on the government. In fact, when reporters interviewed hundreds of Ethiopian refugees who had fled to a refugee camp in Sudan, not a single person mentioned drought as a major or even secondary cause of the famine.

The two most frequent reasons given for the famine were forced labor on the government's collective farms and imprisonment. According to reporter Arch Puddington, "Despite a desperate need for increased food production, peasants were jailed for such charges as not paying their taxes, resisting the confiscation of land, trading outside government channels, refusing to arrest a neighbor as part of militia duty, working the fields during a political seminar or literacy class (frequently mentioned by refugees), suspicion of assisting an anti-government organization, or publicly objecting to government decisions."

There is no question that the government's massive resettlement efforts in the midst of a severe drought caused the deaths of untold thousands. Puddington and other observers make an even stronger accusation. They believe that the government used the famine as a way to deliberately suppress the Ethiopian people. In Puddington's words, "Ethiopia has suffered not so much a natural catastrophe as a deliberate, state-sponsored atrocity."

If these observers are to be believed, the government of Ethiopia intentionally caused millions of people to starve to death. They did this as a way to weaken opposition and tighten their hold on power. Mengistu and other Dergue leaders have denied this, but they do say publicly that violence and killing are part of the necessary struggle to maintain power.

When the famine was over, the government of Ethiopia acknowledged that the suffering had been great. But it promised that better times were ahead for the survivors. Its social revolution, government leaders proclaimed, would lead to a brighter future for all Ethiopians. Whether this will come to pass is much in doubt.

# Six

# Ethiopia's Future

The famine that killed more than one million people between 1983 and 1985 did not just disappear overnight. The rains may have brought temporary relief, but they did not wash away any of Ethiopia's long-term problems. Its farms remained unproductive. Although the government continued to spend 95 percent of its agricultural budget running collective farms, these farms continued to fail miserably. In 1987, they produced only 6 percent of the nation's food.

The rainy seasons of 1985 and 1986 kept famine at bay, but they were years filled with civil strife for Ethiopia. During the brief rest from famine, more and more people voiced their anger at the government. Many demanded Mengistu's resignation. Others tried to overthrow him violently. The People's Liberation Front carried out armed attacks on government resettlement sites, government trucks, and other public facilities. Rebels in Eritrea and Ogaden resumed their struggle for secession. Without a famine to quiet its opponents, the government increased its military actions against them.

Then came 1987, when Ethiopia recorded the lowest single year of rainfall in more than a century. The state of the country's food supply was so fragile that the dry season started yet another famine.

In many parts of Ethiopia, especially the province of Tigre, the famine was nearly as bad as in 1985. In fact, food production was lower in 1987 than it had been in more than ten years. Once again, caravans of starving people wandered the countryside in search of a bag of flour or a handful of beans that would keep them going for a few more days or weeks. Again, the cries of misery rose up across the countryside. Scrawny Ethiopian children, nothing but flesh and bone and swollen stomachs, appeared once more in newsmagazines and television reports around the world. And once again, the cry went out for a massive aid campaign like the one of 1985.

The famine of 1987 and 1988 was not as bad as the one two years earlier. The reasons, however, had nothing to do with any changes within Ethiopia itself. The only difference was that the world community responded more quickly.

Inside Ethiopia, the greatest obstacle to the relief effort in 1987 was

civil strife. During the earlier famine, the rebels and the relief agencies had a mutual understanding. They did nothing to jeopardize one another's efforts. In 1987, however, many rebel groups resented the way the government tried to control food distribution and use it as a weapon. They were furious that the government could force people to comply with its resettlement program or other demands by promising them food. In retaliation, rebel guerrillas attacked trucks belonging to the United Nations and other international agencies delivering food to the hungry.

## Fighting the Rebels

The government, for its part, seemed more concerned with putting down rebellion than feeding the hungry. A frustrated American aid official said, "I'll tell you what the government's three priorities are: fighting the rebels, fighting the rebels, and fighting the rebels."

With this state of civil unrest within the country and the Mengistu government in power, it is difficult to foresee anything but more pain and suffering for the Ethiopian people in the coming years. It may be, however, that the government will change, and that someday one more responsive to the needs of its people will emerge.

Any government with a chance of succeeding in Ethiopia must address the problems and conditions that cause famine. Only then will it rid the country of starvation for good, instead of waiting for the next famine and then relying on international relief efforts. To prevent the recurrence of famine, the nation must improve its population distribution, farming methods, transportation and communications systems, medical care, and education facilities.

## Symptoms of Overpopulation

A resettlement program might help Ethiopia improve the population distribution. The northern regions of Ethiopia have been overfarmed. The great deforestation and desert expansion in that area are symptoms of overpopulation. A gradual, and humane, approach to resettling people in the south may help Ethiopians take better advantage of their resources. Whether collective farming is the way to develop these areas is questionable. Wherever it has been forced on people, it has failed.

A new approach to farming must also be taken to find solutions to the deforestation, erosion, soil depletion, and overgrazing problems that now plague northern Ethiopia. To prevent erosion, farmers may develop soil conservation methods now being tested in the United States and other developed countries. These methods include planting crops between rows of new, fast-growing trees. The roots of these trees help hold the moisture in the ground and prevent erosion. Another way to reduce erosion is to leave the stocks of grain in the ground after harvest instead of clearing them out of the soil. Their roots help combat erosion, and the stalks make excellent fodder for grazing animals.

The best way to maintain fertile soil is to practice mixed cropping. By planting two or more different crops in the same field, or alternating crops from year to year, farmers can make sure that different kinds of nutrients in the soil are being used. Mixed crops allow the various nutrients to periodically replenish themselves. Mixed cropping is also a good form of insurance for the farmer. If a specific plant blight or a particularly harmful infestation of insects occurs, it will usually affect one crop more than the rest. This way, the farmer will be able to harvest at least some of his crops at the end of the growing season.

Irrigation is another way that farmers can increase their productivity. Some Ethiopian farmers are already experimenting with a modified irrigation system called water-trapping. With this method, seeds are planted in ridges that form the banks of small ditches. These ditches trap rainwater in areas where it can be collected and used. By conserving water and soil, and by opening new regions to farming, Ethiopian farmers may someday be able to feed their country's entire population, even during droughts.

Large families were considered a sign of wealth in Ethiopia. Now, the government is trying to control population growth until the country can produce enough food for its citizens.

Producing enough food, however, will be possible only if population growth is controlled. In the past, large families have been considered a sign of wealth in Ethiopia and in most of Africa. Today, the people must be educated instead about the value of birth control. The Mengistu government has already begun to do this. It conducted the first thorough, national census in Ethiopia's history. It intends to repeat this process every ten years so that population growth can be monitored.

If famine does break out again, government leaders will have to respond more quickly and effectively than they have in the past. To do this, they must be able to analyze weather data and forecast droughts in specific areas. If a drought can be anticipated, officials can distribute surplus food and supplies to these areas. In addition, agricultural experts must collect data on the size of the harvest from one year to the next so they can anticipate food shortages.

Finally, Ethiopians must improve the transportation within their country. Their system of roads remains among the worst in the entire world. As long as the people in the countryside are isolated and the roads are poor, Ethiopia will remain backward and susceptible to famine. All other efforts to modernize the country and arm it against the threat of famine will fall short until its systems of transportation and communication are improved.

Once improvements are made in these areas, it will become feasible

Many villages remain isolated by poor roads. Most villagers travel by foot or with the assistance of animals.

Ethiopia's future lies in the hands of its young people, who face numerous difficult challenges.

to build hospitals and schools where all citizens can get to them. It is in the schools that the real hope for the future of Ethiopia lies. For that is where Ethiopians will find their doctors, scientists, businesspeople, politicians, transportation and communication engineers, to lead them into the twenty-first century.

The future of Ethiopia is in the hands of its young people. If those who survived the worst famine in modern history have the determination to learn what must be done and the strength to do it, then the day will come when famine is merely an awful memory in Ethiopia and not a constant threat.

# Glossary

**aristocracy:** A system of government in which the nobility, or the landowning class, rules.

*bega:* The dry season, lasting from September until June.

**collective farm:** A state-owned and -operated farm on which several farmers work the land together for the common good.

**communism:** An economic system in which all people share property, the means of production, and goods produced in common.

**deforestation:** The removal of trees or forests from an area of land.

**Dergue:** The military committee of leaders who ruled Ethiopia after the overthrow of Emperor Haile Selassie.

**drought:** A prolonged period of dry weather.

**ecology:** The relationship among living things and the conditions that surround them.

**famine:** A great lack of food that causes starvation throughout a wide region.

**feudalism:** The political and economic organization in which owning land is a privilege granted by one noble person to another in return for loyalty and military service.

*injera:* A pancakelike bread made from a variety of grains.

*kakat:* Meeting room in the house of a tribal elder.

*k'amis:* Traditional cotton gown or undergarment worn by Ethiopian women.

*kremt:* Rainy season.

**malnutrition:** The unhealthy condition of the body caused by not having enough food.

**militia:** A group of citizens who are not regular soldiers but get some military training for service in an emergency.

**nobility:** The small minority of wealthy landowners with special titles or rank assigned by royalty.

**nomad:** A member of a tribe of people who have no fixed home but keep moving about looking for food, or pasture for their animals.

**Oromo:** The largest ethnic group in Ethiopia.

**resettlement:** A program to relocate a large segment of a population.

**secessionists:** Individuals residing in a region of a country who wish to be independent of that country.

**semiarid:** Having light rainfall, usually less than ten inches per year.

*shamma:* Traditional garment worn by Ethiopian villagers.

**silt:** Particles of soil floating in, or deposited by, rivers and streams.

*tukul:* A house with a thatched roof and walls.

*wat:* A spicy vegetable stew.

*wusa:* A bread made from the pulp of the false banana plant.

*zawya:* House of the dead; a place where bodies are prepared for burial.

# Suggestions for Further Reading

Abebe, Daniel, *Ethiopia in Pictures*. Minneapolis: Lerner Publications Company, 1988.

Arias, Ron, "Ethiopia Now," *People Magazine,* January 13, 1986.

Bennett, R., "Anatomy of a Famine," *Reader's Digest,* May 1985.

Brauman, L., "Famine Aid: Were We Duped?" *Reader's Digest,* October 1986.

Deressa, Yonas, "Free Ethiopia: Rebel Aid," *National Review,* April 24, 1987.

Edmunds, I.G., *Ethiopia: Land of the Conquering Lion of Judah*. New York: Holt Rinehart and Winston, 1975.

Fradin, Dennis Brindell, *Enchantment of the World: Ethiopia*. Chicago: Childrens Press, 1988.

Friedrich, Otto, "Does Helping Really Help?" *Time,* December 21, 1987.

Iyer, Pico, "The Politics of Famine: A Ruthless Regime Compounds the Plight of the Starving," *Time,* May 20, 1985.

Karlen, N., "The Deadly Politics of African Aid Efforts," *Newsweek,* June 3, 1985.

Kaula, Edna Mason, *The Land and the People of Ethiopia*. Philadelphia: J.B. Lippincott, 1972.

Perl, Lila, *Ethiopia: Land of the Lion*. New York: William Morrow and Company, 1972.

Puddington, Arch, "Ethiopia: The Communist Uses of Famine," *Commentary,* April 1986.

Sellassie, Sahle, *Shinega's Village: Scenes of Ethiopian Life*. Berkeley: University of California Press, 1964.

*Time,* "Creeping Coup," July 15, 1974.

*Time,* "Flight from Fear: Behind the Famine, the Grim Outline of a Strategy to Win a Civil War," January 21, 1985.

*Time,* "Twin Plagues of War and Famine," March 28, 1988.

Trimble, J., "Rain and Aid Save Millions of Africans for Now," *U.S. News & World Report,* January 20, 1986.

*U.S. News & World Report,* "Starvation Watch," April 25, 1988.

# Works Consulted

Brown, L.R., "Will the Rains Return to Africa?" *International Wilderness,* December 1985.

Charen, Mona, "Quick Fix Humanitarianism," *National Review,* June 28, 1985.

*Economist,* "Drought Still Means Hunger," September 27, 1975.

Fenton, J., "Ethiopia: Victors and Victims," *New York Review of Books,* November 7, 1985.

Harris, Myles F., *Breakfast in Hell.* New York: Poseidon Press, 1987.

Hofen, A., "The Origins of Famine," *New Republic,* January 21, 1985.

Holden, C., "Did Aid Speed an Inevitable Upheaval?" *Science,* October 27, 1974.

Humphreys, N.K., "Ethiopia: Trapped by Foreign Aid," *The Nation,* June 1973.

Kerr, R.A., "Fifteen Years of African Drought," *Science,* March 22, 1985.

Koehn, P., "Ethiopian Politics: Military Intervention and Prospects for Future Change," *Africa Today,* April 1975.

Murphy, J.S., "Innocent Emperor: Ethiopia Exploits Itself," *The Nation,* September 14, 1974.

Posner, M., "Harsh Rule in an Arid Land," *MacLeans,* May 19, 1986.

Raloff, J., "Africa's Famine: The Human Dimension," *Science News,* May 11, 1985.

Raloff, J. and Weisburd, S., "Climate and Africa: Why the Land Goes Dry," *Science News,* May 4, 1985.

Schwab, Peter, *Ethiopia: Politics, Economics and Society.* Boulder, CO: Lynne Rienner Publishers, Inc., 1985.

Thomas, Maria, "A State of Permanent Revolution: Ethiopia Bleeds Red," *Harper's,* January 1987.

Tierney, J., "Drought in Africa: The Bigger Picture," *Science,* April 1985.

Tucker, J., "In Ethiopia, Food Is a Weapon," *The Nation,* February 8, 1986.

Tucker, J., "The Politics of Famine in Ethiopia," *The Nation,* January 19, 1985.

Wolf, E.C., "Once Fertile Fields in Ethiopia's Highlands May Be Abandoned in Next Decade," *Natural History,* April 1986.

# Index

# About the Author and Illustrator

**The Author,** Elizabeth S. Glaser, a Minnesota native, has ten years of writing experience. After graduating summa cum laude from Moorhead State University in 1980 with degrees in English and Mass Communications, she won a variety of state and national awards as a news reporter. She also has experience in the areas of marketing, advertising and corporate communications, winning awards for creativity and writing style. Glaser currently is the editor-in-chief for Center for Management Systems, a national newsletter publishing group based in northwestern Iowa.

**The Illustrator**, Brian McGovern, has been active in both fine art and commercial illustration for twenty years. His recent clients include AT&T, DuPont, Harvey's Lake Tahoe, and Chase Manhattan Bank. He has exhibited paintings in San Francisco and New York and was recently a published winner in *American Artists Magazine* in the "Preserving Our National Wilderness" competition. He has won several Best of Show awards in the fantasy art field and the 1987 Distinguished Leadership Award from American Biographical Institute in North Carolina.

# Picture Credits

## DATE DUE

| | | | |
|---|---|---|---|
| | | | |
| | | | |
| | | | |
| | | | |
| | | | |
| | | | |
| | | | |
| | | | |
| | | | |
| | | | |
| | | | |
| | | | |

CHAVEZ HIGH SCHOOL
LIBRARY
HOUSTON, TEXAS